THE PARLIAMENT OF IDIOTS:
TRYST OF THE *SINATORS*

POEMS

Kraftgriots

Also in the series (POETRY)

David Cook et al: *Rising Voices*
Olu Oguibe: *A Gathering Fear*, winner, 1992 All Africa Okigbo prize for Literature & Honourable mention, 1993 Noma Award for Publishing in Africa
Nnimmo Bassey: *Patriots and Cockroaches*
Okinba Launko: *Dream-Seeker on Divining Chain*
Onookome Okome: *Pendants*; winner, 1993 ANA/Cadbury poetry prize
Nnimmo Bassey: *Poems on the Run*
Ebereonwu: *Suddenly God was Naked*
Tunde Olusunle: *Fingermarks*
Joe Ushie: *Lambs at the Shrine*
Chinyere Okafor: *From Earth's Bedchamber*
Ezenwa Ohaeto: *The Voice of the Night Masquerade*; joint-winner, 1997 ANA/Cadbury poetry prize
George Ehusani: *Fragments of Truth*
Remi Raji: *A Harvest of Laughters*; joint-winner, 1997 ANA/Cadbury poetry prize
Patrick Ebewo: *Self-Portrait & Other Poems*
George Ehusani: *Petals of Truth*
Nnimmo Bassey: *Intercepted*
Joe Ushie: *Eclipse in Rwanda*
Femi Oyebode: *Selected Poems*
Ogaga Ifowodo: *Homeland & Other Poems*, winner, 1993 ANA poetry prize
Godwin Uyi Ojo: *Forlorn Dreams*
Tanure Ojaide: *Delta Blues and Home Songs*
Niyi Osundare: *The Word is an Egg* (2000)
Tayo Olafioye: *A Carnival of Looters* (2000)
Ibiwari Ikiriko: *Oily Tears of the Delta* (2000)
Francis A. Odiniya: *The Traveller with Two Souls* (2000)
Arnold Udoka: *I am the Woman* (2000)
Akinloye Ojo: *In Flight* (2000)
Joe Ushie: *Hill Songs* (2000)
Ebereonwu: *The Insomniac Dragon* (2000)
Deola Fadipe: *I Make Pondripples* (2001)
Remi Raji: *Webs of Remembrance* (2001)
'Tope Omoniyi: *Farting Presidents and Other Poems* (2001)
Tunde Olusunle: *Rhythm of the Mortar* (2001)
Abdullahi Ismaila: *Ellipsis* (2001)

THE PARLIAMENT OF IDIOTS:
TRYST OF THE *SINATORS*

POEMS

Tayo Olafioye

kraftgriots

Published by
Kraft Books Limited
6A Polytechnic Road, Sango, Ibadan
Box 22084, University of Ibadan Post Office
Ibadan, Oyo State, Nigeria
& 234 (2) 8106655
E-mail: kraftbooks@yahoo.com
krabooks@onebox.com

© Tayo Olafioye 2002

First published 2002

ISBN 978-039-059-6

= KRAFTGRIOTS =
(A literary imprint of Kraft Books Limited)

All Rights Reserved

First printing, June 2002

Dedication

To my troika of executive siblings whom I love very dearly, so that they may live forever in human consciousness.

Olu Olafioye — Of Obafemi Awolowo Foundation in Lagos. Retired Librarian of the National Library, Lagos.

Obafemi Olayeye — First cousin. A classicist. Retired Principal, Teachers' College, Ode Aye

Ademola Olayeye — Eldest of all. First cousin Retired Assistant Director of Education, Ministry of Education, Lagos State.

Gratitude

Kunle Olafioye of Igbotako, Oshoro in Ikaleland; Tunde Lawal: Kwara Poly — Ilorin; and Tunde Asaju — *Newswatch,* Abuja; Jamie Anne Guerina, San Diego; for being my research assistants over the years.

Disclaimer

This narrative and historical document of events by no means reflect the representative national conclave. Men and women of conscience and integrity seek to fulfil its mission. They passionately and sincerely demonstrate their concern about the welfare of the state.

By *The Parliament of Idiots*, I mean its constituency of offenders and those who by tacit or explicit commission participate in this particular scandal under review and/or any other lapses not yet exposed.

Any parliament of angels proves impossible to constitute but so long its moral pollutions are very limited. This poet remains a realist.

Tayo

Preface

The Parliament of Idiots ... is a remarkable collection — sad, ominous, dreadful, and passionate. It is a paradoxical mixture of the tremours of an anguished soul and the zealous clamours of a dejected patriot. Olafioye personally mourns the death of his mother as he agonizes over the 'passing' of his nation, Nigeria — the giant of the African continent reduced to a paltry midget. Throughout the collection there is the criss-crossing of the moods of personal sorrow and the tragedy of the traumatised collective soul of a nation. In his words: "Today, I mourn the death of my two mothers: my biological mother Elizabeth Kehinde, and my natal mother, Nigeria, a motherland to which my heart belongs.

Then when I was visiting my natural mother, the death or dishonour and besmirching of my natal mother, Nigeria, doubly ravaged my heart. The probe of the Senate leaders and the impeachment that ensued exposed the betrayal of polity which meant the asphyxiation of this young democracy, my motherland, my Nigeria. This primal land gave birth to us, and many of us own no other to which we intuitively belong."

This collection must stir the hearts and souls of truly 'concerned' Nigerians. Some of the poems are rendered in parables; but their structural unity, and hypnotic recall of the events of history establish Tayo Olafioye not only as a poet of substance, but also as a sensitive and perceptive observer of the life and socio-political events in the Nigerian nation. The allegorical 'story' introduced in the poem, "Azikiwe's Curse" is told in full ramifications in the poems: "The Disobedient Fowl", "Ogidan — The Mountain Lion", "Christmas Bonus: In the Songhai Sinate", and "The Impeachment". So incensed is Olafioye with his subject that in "The Disobedient Fowl", the disguised 'Chube Ogidan' is not difficult to decode. But Olafioye's literary technique seems to be to make his language and imagery easily accessible such that the culprits in the Nigerian political arena will be hard to miss.

This is a collection that seeks to tell it all; to bare it all, and to unmask the masquerades in Nigerian contemporary leadership and governance.

Olafioye is at his best in his sensitive depiction of the foibles of Nigeria and Nigerians. Consider the import of such poems as "Credentials", "Minimum wage: maximum wahala", "Okada motorscooters", "Book launching", "Birthday card for my country", "The Songhai nation", and "College without convenience". (How does a government committed to social welfare establish an institution of higher learning in this day and age, and not consider toilet as an essential facility?) In spite of the encircling physical, spiritual and metaphysical rottenness, Olafioye is still able to afford some effusive humour as in the poem "The African time". But Olafioye does not spare even himself a few jabs as in "Homecoming", "Don't call me daddy", and particularly "The alien plant" where the joke is on his hair. Every social event, every national event exposes the hypocrisy, empty aggrandizement, and falsehood in Nigeria and Nigerians, with the highest debauchery evident in "A Tryst of the Sinators".

The Parliament of Idiots ... is food for thought for all Nigerians. The soul of the nation seems to have collapsed precipitating among other things, the exodus of some of the best brains in Nigeria. From the various corners of the globe where they find themselves, they give vent to their nostalgic emotions in poetry, prose of various types and drama. In these they reprimand, castigate, lampoon, satirize, and cajole their homeland, its people and their national and cultural idiosyncrasies and maladies; defying the sanctity of not singing the unpalatable dirges in a foreign land. But they are neither traitors nor 'sell-outs'. Through these new types of fiction, African literature is progressively being redefined; frontiers are emerging into the fold, new directions are hoisted on the horizon. The African 'story' now can be told (and is being told) with authenticity and unparalleled integrity from home and abroad. Tayo Olafioye's *The Parliament of Idiots* is an inimitable example of a Nigeria tale told from afar but possessing all the ingredients of a home-crafted masterpiece.

The collection might make some Nigerians laugh, but one hopes that it will also make all Nigerians think about our purpose as a nation in the 21st century, our sense of direction as a race, and the true meaning of patriotism and national service in our land. Can we truly say that our elected or appointed leaders are indeed serving the interests of the people they represent or claim to represent? Our national grief can no longer be blamed on the exploits of the colonial foreigner. It can now be laid squarely on our own evil doing, and the frightening nonchallant acceptance of our inglorious national sodomy as a divine heritage, immutable, and irreversible. Listen to Tayo Olafioye in "The conclave of hyenas":

> Once aliens devastated our shores
> Their bones lay in our soil
> Formed the rivers of ashes underneath
> Now, the internal antagonists
> Are the locusts that ruin the crops.
> They mat the acreage with their underbellies
> They too will die from the heat of the earth.

The Parliament of Idiots ... is a must for all Nigerians concerned about the survival of Nigeria as a nation to be reckoned with in the 21st century. The truth is not always sweet but it must be told. Tayo Olafioye is not only an accomplished poet that all lovers of literature should hail, he also has earned his place on the HONOUR roll of Nigerians at home or abroad who place their country before self; who can be counted on to stand by their sense of unwavering integrity and true patriotism without counting the cost.

Prof. Ernest N. Emenyonu
St. Augustine's College, Raleigh, North Carolina, USA

A Filial appreciation of a mother's death

These past few years constituted a turning point in my life. After forty, anything becomes possible. A cancer of the prostate, followed a few months later by a stroke, devastated me. I survived both with effective surgeries without chemotherapy or radiology. I remain a full man. Brain surgery with angioplasty stenting lifted the stroke threat. I am normal again. The account of these double whammy attacks within a few months gave birth to my narrative — A STROKE OF HOPE—that alerted the reading world what dying felt like. I also etched the work from my hospital bed as a legacy to bequeath my little girl — nine years old at the time — a document of what might have killed me, so that she might know what afflicted her father and how I might have passed on.

The strength of surviving these two serious visitations, my publishers and friends egged me to return home, to launch the six new works I managed to do at the time. I had left home eleven years before without a visceral reunion with my roots. Less fortunate candidates could have succumbed to any of these afflictions, so to live to tell about them deserved a festival of gratitude to my spiritual universe, ancestors, all the unseen and inexplicable entities. They knew why I endured and grew. My profound gratitude also extends to the American medical ingenuities and their providers. Without them, where would I have been?

I made the triumphant return home to raving reviews and acclaim. I could not have received a warmer welcome and appreciation. However, behind such ceremony, was lurking the next strange happening in my life. I have encountered many. My mother felt no joy when she saw me in Lagos. What came back home to her was not her vibrant son, the professor, who had left home some years before, but his ghost. Gaunt, scowly, jowly-jawed, emaciated, and dehydrated, a ripe candidate for expiration. I showed her the face of death, not mine. My countenance scared me too; a scarecrow, grimaced back at me from my pictures in the newspapers. All my families harried and feared the worst, especially my mother. Happily, however, death does not visit all who lie sick laden in bed.

I am her first-born. Telepathically, she concluded that I was going to die before her, given the gravity and ghoulish image. She became quietly determined that such an unnatural tragedy would not happen in her lifetime. She refused to plant her adult son in the grave before her time. I could read the fright in her eyes, as she complained bitterly daily about my comatose kinetic dynamics.

She was living her retirement years with my sister in Lagos. My condition formed their menu of daily conversations. Days before my return to the United States, I paid her my last visit. We enjoyed a good time of warm and hearty family chats. I never suspected this closeness knowing that it would be the last.

After some hours, I stood to take my leave. My mother and sister walked me to the front yard. Strangely, my mother chose not to look at me as we walked to the car. Transfixed, she looked at the ground at her feet. She screwed up her face into a determined grimace. My heart thundered, telling me that my mother was going through a transformation. She did not wave a goodbye. She did not look up. She did not say a word. She did not move an inch until my car diminished out of her sight. For that symbolic omen, I knew that an ominous stroke was going to mark me before the year 2000, ran out. The blow did not take long. Three weeks after I returned to America, the phone rang in the dark to wake me up in San Diego. The weeping voice of my younger brother from London announced: "Mother died this morning, 6 a.m. Lagos time." Possibly, my mother died of old age, of natural causes, but the circumstance of her death lent itself to cultural interpretations.

I felt a bolt strike me from the depth of my being. I knew right away, metaphysically, that my mother had died my death. She had willed herself to die. She had called to herself a death of self-sacrifice. My sister reported to me where my mother chose to be buried . She had not sickened, she did not suffer, even a cold or fever. On the eve of her death, she had asked my sister to pray for her. She went to bed. At 5 a.m., she woke my sister up to ask her for a bath. My sister gave her one. That was my mother's last ritual. At 6 a.m., she lay dead. For now, only absence connects between us.

Most of the western world may not understand or believe that cultural deaths exist except metaphysical deaths. We Africans paint life with cultural artifacts, the cosmos of spirits, totems, national struggles and accepted beliefs, most of which best transmit the African writer's message because of familiarity or well-known imagistic references and assimilation. We are still rich in virgin happenings to write about, not daffodils or Mt. Rushmore, or the mighty Mississippi or the legacy of the Nazis. For the most part, Western literary conceptions no longer have such ethnic resources any more to rely upon. They revel in the post-modern modernist literary consciousness. They dwell in the new worlds of intertextualities, computers, Internet, astrophysics, cinematography, space exploration and the like, as their environments alert them. What serious African writer would want to imitate any western style of writing, good or bad? We float in the world of virgin materials that best inform our creativity. They flounder in the world of cosmetics. We swim in the world of pristine spirits and metaphysics; theirs bear no names. What they say or think little matters. The African chronicler must stay true to his environment to remain relevant. He must breathe typically African atmospheres while he reaches out to touch the universal. He cannot afford to commit a cultural incest or to lock himself into a refrigerator; he must maintain a measure of cultural and environmental affinity and fidelity.

In my Yoruba cultural totem, a mother's life conclusion is successful when her children outlive her to perform funeral obsequies over her. In death a mother or father wears richly ornamented traditional clothing, hand woven in the heirloom. Through this particular fabric of red and purple outlay, is an Alaari: A proverbial profundity weaves: "My child, when I pass on, please drape me with an Alaari outfit." This choice of cloth carries a cultural significance. This traditional flag of recognition and of life's success up — drapes a parent. My mother wanted that rite and I am pleased that she received her earned reward. As our culture recognizes it, a parent to whom his or her children give a fitting burial, wears the mantle of a successful parenthood.

I am also pleased that she died a decent death: no prolonged illness, not even for a day. I am glad that she last saw me. That remained her wish, one that always marked the last paragraph in her letters, "to see you again before I answer the call of my fathers." My mother died the death of honor, a sacrificial death. She did not want to witness the death of her grown child, not only a nightmarish tragedy but also a cultural disgrace, a cultural taboo. This disgrace, an "ofo," an utmost cultural tragedy, imposes itself upon her as she understood and accepted the label. Unimaginable, this burden looms psychologically perilous to lift. I am well again incidentally, bouncy and alive. My mother died for me. With her spiritual tunnel vision, she will watch over my siblings and me. I so pray and believe.

Today, I mourn the death of my two mothers: my biological mother Elizabeth Kehinde, and my natal mother, Nigeria, a motherland to which my heart belongs. Then when I was visiting my natural mother, the death or dishonor and besmirching of my natal mother, Nigeria, doubly ravaged my heart. The probe of the senate leaders and the impeachment that ensued exposed the betrayal of polity which meant the asphyxiation of this young democracy, my motherland, my Nigeria. This primal land gave birth to us, and many of us own no other to which we intuitively belong. To see her through this deathly elder-abuse at the hands of a few prodigal sons and daughters, gave me the creeps, the scars of the heart and a thorned, smashed soul. These thankless children drank up her honey of dreams and milk of societal regeneration, through financial irregularities and deep-seated insensitivity. Not only these are to blame but also, those who pretentiously and facetiously put up stances of innocence.

Such elegiac musings that bled the heart of this poet gave rise to the chronicling of these narrative monodies and threnodies: *The Parliament of Idiots: Tryst of the Sinators.*

San Diego, California
2001

Introduction

African poets have long come to realize that they need new themes for their new creations. Independence since Ghana (1957) was a watershed. Gone are the yesterdays of anti-colonial attacks and their corollary, nationalism. Nor did this latter mood last long once the seventies set in. Back, then a new tyranny had already set up its throne, making itself comfortable. The stage was set for political self-destruction: military rule, dictatorship, greed, imprisonment, preventive detention, executions. After the Nigerian civil war, Wole Soyinka was asking, "Where are all the followers gone?" In so many countries, not least Nigeria, poverty, plundering of national resources, exile of political enemies, civil war overtook the continent: all this in the midst of want, ignorance, diseases.

The new voices, such as Tayo Olafioye, are a clear example of the break with the idyllic verses Africa was singing. In high political times and fiery nationalism, Africans had to find spiritual leverage against white rule and reaffirm their cultural togetherness. Suddenly, the stuff of post-colonial poetry had to find a new language, mood and goals for a new kind of urgency: home-grown political tyranny. The pastoral lyricism of yesterday has all but petered out. There is now a voice in the present-day modes that makes itself heard. It makes for a dramatic tension in the poetry suggesting a dialogue between poet and a political Other. The enemy is no longer simply white rule and the colonising aspects of Christianity. We are under native elites propped up by the former colonial power as mere compradors. This breed is the real and visible enemy: the man who was my schoolmate, with whom I shared living space, and the banter and bustle and adventures of youth.

Yet political tyranny is not the only theme, as we find in our present collection. The tender moments of family reunions; speculations about dying; remembrance of kinder days gone by, kinder days of the present; marital bliss ... The poet let us share the landscape of his mind-states as he travels from place to place from his base San Diego, California; the shifting states of mind in a restless soul.

All these features come to us assertively — in a driving diction. A compelling diction with muscle and enthusiasm. We observe in the process of his search for a resolution emotional centre that stays in charge of the poet's diction. The verse keeps rolling on, wave after wave. It conjures up in our minds the image of a night traveller drawn irresistibly to a distant light flickering in the distance: on and on and on, drawn towards some resolution. Distances are an illusion in the dark. No sooner does the goal appear within reach than the footsteps seem never-ending.

Thus there is in Olafioye's exploration of his shifting states of mind an air of unfinished business. Yet the wholeness of each poem is not necessarily sacrificed. I always find intriguing in poetry, rather than the appearance of a finality. We read about his visit — after the first ten years, to his native Nigeria, where he finds himself in the presence of his mother. He tells us about her subsequent death; about meeting his grandma, "contentment dancing across his face": "one with children never dies". He experiences moments of "shocking delight"... "If you were a star/ We would have stayed in the galaxy with you ..." "To carry the flags of memory ..." "My absence has been/The only connection between us to date..."

The poet's travels keep his sensibilities quivering with the compulsion to articulate memory. An experience only the person knows who is living away from his loved ones, his roots. You cling to memory as your lifeline. Wherever you go, if you have your pores and eyes constantly open, you register disparate "architects of the mind". Don't ever let go of that lifeline — memory. Poetry, whether in the form of verse, fiction, drama, becomes a medium of therapy. He invokes the essence of poetry in his ritual of reaffirmation of his origins, anchored in ancestral presences and their enduring companionship and protection. The meeting point between the condition of exile and self-fulfilment. Another compulsion: concern over the tragedy that Nigeria had become, since the civil strife of the sixties of the last century. Politician become millionaire, Abacha, was only an active extension and invalid of a post-traumatic condition that continues to dog the country. Olafioye's driving diction registers the rumblings and gloom of recent years. "In the crevice of time/All darkness and no sun/..." "Endemic auras of sadness/Wicked thoughts unspeakable..." His consolation? "Life breathes even on the dung heaps"....

Of course we have been here before in Olafioye's previous collections: *Arrowheads to my Heart* (1999); *A Carnival of Looters; A Stroke of Hope; Ubangiji* — all three in 2000. The images of conflict, of unease continue to vibrate in us: "The cyclone of depravity ... Auschwitz sounds a millennium ago ... Carnivals of decadence...." "How do you pray for hope/a nation ruled by demons/with hairs in their teeth ..." "The beast; amidst us/ Scavenged dung heaps for cadavers"; ... "To stay the reign of /The most satanic pope of Islam/...The Khalif of ritual death/Called abacha of Nigeria...

Not all shade by any means, though. After a heroic recovery from illness, Olafioye's search, we are reassured, will yet find resolution. Never absolute, even at that; yet we know he has the unflagging energy to keep renewing self.

Es'kia Mphahlele
Writer, Professor Emeritus
Doyen of African Literature
Lebowakgomo,
Limpopo Province
South Africa

Contents

Dedication 5
Gratitude 6
Disclaimer 7
Preface 8
A filial appreciation of a mother's death 11
Introduction 15

I: THE SKY CAN'T KEEP ITS SECRETS

One day 22
Azikiwe's curse 23
The conclave of hyenas 24
Minimum wage: maximum wahala 26
A tail of discomforts 28
Christmas bonus: in the Songhai Sinate 30
Crows of the roach 31
Ogidan — the mountain lion 33
The iinpeachment 36
The disobedient fowl 40
Gbajumo 41
Birthday card for my country 42
The Songhai nation 43
Mantras of the mafiosi 44
Credentials 45
Debt relief mystique 46
News-channel 10 47
A tryst of the *Sinators* 48

II: THE SOUL IS FOREVER LONGING

Three architects of the mind 50
Homecoming 51
Okada motorscooters 53
An invincible melancholy 54
Feel me with your eyes 55
Book launching 57
The facetious appeal 58

Don't call me daddy 60
Tijuana hearts of mercy 61
Veronica Howard 63
Indira Mann 64
Folake & Jummy Bamigboye 65
Akinnurun: the man of thunder 66
Dorcas Ogunro: the Lubokun matriarchy 68
The alien plant 69
Musa Na'Allah: an alley cat with eight lives left 70

III: WHOEVER DESPIES SMALL THINGS HAS NEVER BEFORE STEPPED ON A SCORPION

Wanted 74
College without convenience 75
A marital college 77
The iron-hearted 78
George's love 79
Ximena Munoz 80
Philosophic inscriptions on Songhai buses 81
The african time 82
For Tayo Olafioye 83
Beauty on water 84
Prisoners of history 86

Synopsis: The Year 2000 in Nigeria 89

I

The Sky Can't Keep Its Secrets

One day

One day I'll sail the troubled seas
Using my heart as a compass.

Someday I'll rid the world of AIDS
Using my songs as a prescription.

Someday I'll raid the governance of stench
Using my poems as bombs.

Someday I'll wipe the world of leprosy
Using my art of poetry.

Someday I'll slaughter the whales of diseases
Using my pens as harpoons.

Someday I'll poach tribalism called racism
Using my works as arrows.

Someday I'll forge a true nation
Using my umbrella of the rainbow.

One day I'll unite the world
Using the language of humanity

United Nations Headquarters, New York, New York

Azikiwe's curse

It was from the tongue of Edoni*
That the hyena earned
The curse of irascibility:
Always youthful and strong but intemperate
His volcanic bursts:
The language of mental dysfunction
If we fish intensely
We would find a crippled fish.
Any repair, too late
Do not tangle with the spirits
Only an oracle could dance
To their drums.

Schiphol International Airport, Amsterdam, Holland

---

* Edoni — a 13th century Benin Monarch.

The conclave of hyenas

They sheared the elephant*:
Arms, legs, and limbs
Flesh, carcass, and tusks.
Its heart gulped in a flash
The foxes provided for themselves
And over gorged their esophagus
Like dogs they barked backwards
Not seeing their fronts.
They played the lions,
And wildebeests without tails.
These tribal hyenas–
The G5: Lagido*, Heirat
Adan, Ikoko* and Ikeregbe*–
Laid the royal bed
That cushioned Ogidan's bones
They were the chambermaids of horror
In the hierarchy of poli-prostitution
The contract scam:
A festival of smut from above
All germinated
The murk sub conscious
The odor of the skunk
Followed their trails

Once aliens devastated our shores
Their bones lay in our soil
Formed the rivers of ashes underneath.
Now, the internal antagonists
Are the locusts that ruin the crops.

---

* Elephant — Nigerian national treasury or resources
* Lagido — money
* Ikoko — wolf
* Ikeregbe the goat

They mat the acreage with their underbellies
They too will die from the heat of the earth.

Non-intended corporations
Siphoned away thousand millions:
Cee Chris, Centre & Point, Asso Logistics
All a ruse in technocracy
Many checks posted mystically in accounts
Contracts approved without process
Where possible, they signed with their toes
Laptops by Tritech Computers
Without limit like bonuses without merit.
One should not acquire more
When sharing ill-gotten inheritance.
That the cat can climb and dismount
Make him fall into a ditch.

These idiots really tested the stone
To see if it bled water.
Now they know
Niger stones shed tears and blood.
Any ventriloquist could have
Read such a future for their hopes
No conscience, no logic
No democratic temper-
Their peoples already comatose
Compliment of Abacha's vitrol,
The totalitarian mammon
Whose people, daily like cats,
Eat stone breads for dinner
Voltore, Voltore all,
On the rooftops of our domiciles.

For as long as we have memories
Yesterday shall remain unforgotten.

Lagos

Minimum wage: maximum wahala*

Songhai laborers:
Will never climb
Out of the crypt of misery
Dank all life long.
They are cursed:
Reined in by those they chose
To lift them.
No greater enemy
Than the one, in one's household
The python with which one sleeps
At night on the same bed.
7000 naira* wages, slashed to the bone—
Before the cock crows.
Their fish heads dillied and dallied
What do they care?
The kingfishers of pains.
Their own mints outside the pail
The black gold lubricates
Their fingers—
Bales of the '₦'* notes
Carried by midnight owls
Made pregnant the garments they wear
To make truths face backwards
These law making bandits.
Those accorded titles of dignity
Should avoid perverting the will of the polity.
They forget however,
The sky is flat as the sea.

---

* Wahala — hassle
* Naira — local currency
* '₦' notes — Naira currency notes

Strikes today, famine tomorrow
The Mekunnus* are dying
Talakawas* eye the moon for delivery
Slave machines of penury
Not even a noble austerity assigned them
They ate unhappiness for dinner
The new day can be ancient again—
Of thwarted desires and forlorn hopes
Their work not only sweats but also thinks and panics
Only marauders maim without care.
Amidst the throngs of forthright animals
Lives the fool.
The virus that decimates a plant
Lives amidst its leaves.

Ikeja, Lagos

---

* Mekunnus — ordinary citizen, people without clout
* Talakawas — the poor

A tail of discomforts

No such cocoon exists
The kingfisher in Songhai
Enjoyed perks unimaginable
The rat pretended to be a lion—
A cow that comforts with its tails
The heart of a viper
A bee that stings the dead—
Boundless in dramatics
As if the sun never rises
Limitless in apparatchiks—
12 cars, police escorts
10 vans, burly guards
12 riders, with status horns
20 cars, for area boys, cooks and laundry men
A mansion, the people's sweat
6 doctors for emergencies
In case he caught a cold or dreamed
Some assassins: real or imagined.
What would the super powers display?
A separate consignment at the halfway
In Enugu, in case he needed a rest
In the village.
Abuja, round the clock
Nothing went to sleep there
In case he sneezed from his chain snore
The madam too, her cortege of ghostly fops
The wife of a captain, a captain too.

A velvet revolution of waste and emptiness
Not Ogidan alone
Even if cleared of all puddles and slush
The vultures, tortoises,
Foxes and cobras convene
In their own alliance
In the den of the dead.

The hearts still gashed
With the culture of insensitivity
All the poisoned arrows
And high emptinesses,
This was the decay
That democracy fought
The people aghast!!!
In a land of insufficiency
Where water oozes from the stone.

If you cannot cover kola nuts with more leaves
Do not strip it of the ones already there.
Remember:
He, who over stays at the grave yard,
Must surely see the ghost
Death: their last official performance

Lagos

Christmas bonus: in the Songhai Sinate

Never before has daylight been so dark
The eclipse of the people's innocence
Homeland spirit drenched in hemlock and stench
Rancid all over the sphere
Ogidan, the Sinate patriarch
Harnessed 22 mil naira for his vault
His deputy, Aburaker*, only 17 mil with bravado
Some hefty crumbs for marginal groundlings.
The Songhai worker–
His usual dose of placebos and poverties.

The sinate always manured its farmland
Not the welfare of the masses.
When the fool contracts leprosy
He lives alone in the grove.

One poser though–
How much will Jesus Christ collect
From Songhai tax payers
For his own birthday?

Insensitivity galore, our dance with death
The crows of a new dawn
Disappear faster than that of the roach
Yet none of us would
Leave this planet alive
Despite the ill gotten mounds–
The perceptible grief of my time–
No other angels but our own initiatives
Those without tears
Have no heart.

Agege, Lagos State

---

* Aburaker — one who rakes, pillages; amasses unhealthy profits

Crows of the roach

Ikeregbe's* spittoon
Gave his superiors waves of the brain
Farted lots of putrid
A constantly decaying sludge
His tumor ferments
Puked, at the probe, scams
Never before diagnosed
The landscape drenched in red slush
And blood stained debris
No formaldehyde can
Neutralize the stench.

He sank miles deep
Into the ethical swamp
In this season of political vertigos
Like the eagle above, he forgot to realize
Those below were watching him
Other critters then mooed
They did not understand
The language of deceit
Should not have feared
The heat of the sun
Truth would have blunted
Its intensity.

The he-goat was once a cattle egret
But now, a roach,
Knows no stream of action to swim
But the drools of the mouth
Now he does not know
Where he lost his memory

---

* Ikeregbe — the stubborn goat, goofy and erratic

He that swallows the mortar
Shall forever remain uncomfortable.

The goat bleats in the pen
No one knows why till now
Since grief has no credentials.

The cock that had crowed
Olumo to Aso rock,
Had failed all with
Inadequacy and incompetence
Hence the dyke broke loose.
Every one carved a territory
To dismember the unity.
Our hope is a bird in flight.

Lagos

Ogidan — the mountain lion

His only flaw–
A scholastic naivety–
Usually the bane of swots
As always, he stirred
The calm trees
Forgetting that no creature
Can stay still
In a tornado of lightning.
Imperially slim and nobly endowed,
He glittered when he walked
Elegantly impeccable with a tail whisk
Chiefly accosted, the Oyi–
Humorously human when he testified,
Brilliant like a fox
Who condemns the trap
But not himself.
A mule
Courted by incapacity
For imagination.

His face has felt
The harmattan* howls
When he hid to set a fire
He forgot that
He could not hide the smoke.

The black Mamba, the old whip in the forest
Waited to maul the stray dog
Corruption without end–
The old Mamba had two birth certificates
Each a different date and name

---

* Harmattan — African cold drying wind that usually blows from the Sahara desert from December to March.

Three grammar schools
None which he attended
Even the British Middle Temple
A claim, a cloud, then a tussle.
At this crossroads,
An egg, a kernel and a stone.
Under the Olumo, a hybrid
Of snakes and tortoises

Ogidan let down the sharp knife of his mind
Allowing the massacres in the Savannah
The eagle did not know
What was in the pit

Ogidan once plastered ancestral pillars,
Awo and Zik, with his tongue.
Now he muzzled the Sinate
With brain and abracadabra
Swallowing the decibels of self importance
While nemeses were digging trenches
Under his dome
Contracts flowed the recipes of distort
Like floods through his unsuspecting dykes
I felt his funeral in my heart.

He advertised his brilliance
On the billboards of illusion.
However wise the young,
He cannot be richer
Than the aged in experience.
When delirious with certainty
He forgot the wraths of the departed.
And swelled like an interior sun
In his sugar of vanity
He was oblivious
Of the tortoises under the rock
They concorted honeys of untruths;
By accident as usually happens

They put a political plug
Through his gullet
A probe, an impeachment,
Their irrational exuberance
Our sullen art of mismanagement
Those who killed the domestic animal
Are not our heroes

The curse of the aged
If it dims in the morn
Will assure a hit in the twilight.
The Oyi who stylishly robed
Fell like the waterfall in the Sun
His effort from the beginning
Was the condemnation of fate—
The Emperor has no clothes.
Others: irrational warriors
Of terror.

San Diego, California

The impeachment

"Ogidan impeached"
The papers blared
The elephant has fallen
The king ditched in the abyss
Obalufon* blinked in outrage
Lightning struck in the forest
Bonfires leveled the savannah.
Kipling once said:
"Fame and disaster come
One after the other
Treat them the same, my son."

This has long been coming
When detractors spat his name
As the tobacco phlegm of disgust.
His brinkmanship at large
Earned him the curse of their pains
Actually, the monarch
Started to fall
From the hour of coronation
So mazed their webs of unforgiveness
Only because he wore the cap
Of the sage and the parrot's.
You do not undermine those
Whose maneuvers are
As impure as your own.
They denied him the twilight of existence.

Once giddy with power and illusion
Commandeered the national mace
His staff of office
But the property of the nation

---

* Obalufon — an Ife supreme legendary monarch

Hid it in his village
To douse the embers of plots
To ditch him; they never quit, those
Witches and wizards of pursuit
When will the goat not be sacrificed?
Time will tell and it did
Adroitly played the chess of survival
Used lofty gibbers
To confuse and contuse
The erudition of the press
And his peers in the Sinate.
The home plate like the calabash
Of the pantheons,
Is never known to be wholly clean,
The woods would avenge themselves

When life is rather giddy
One should be careful
No one's love abides
Except that of one's own destiny
Political humpiness or marriage
Never Lasts
Too many ghosts lurking
Behind the bridal suite.

And then, it happened:
The Niger cyclones of sand
The inimical elements that stifle
And blindfolds without regards—
Those who are too smart
Often become victims
Of their own cleverness
Malfeasance, the abuse of office and scams
They charged—
Roasting and decapitating the elephant.
Who is afraid of the Oyi?
Those whose thrones he rattles
—Tornadic force—

Before or in 2003

Awards to selves and cronies
Irregularities in accounts
Unregistered bedfellows, mostly ghosts
Precipitate contract awards without clearance
Signed evidence undeniable
It was the fleecing of the forest
National treasury thus debauched
National projects prodigalized
National assets prostituted
National spirits assassinated–
Crimes against humanity and the dispossessed
Be careful though — the rat-finks
Who wear calico shrouds of falsehood.

This child — democracy —
Or Osundare's 'demoncrazy'
Never always like any other.
Too fragile at this time,
To toss so flippantly
Needs cultural menus of nurture.
The past is a pain-fest
Too fresh to forget
Measures must be taken, ostensibly,
To dam up the flood
Hence the impeachment
Of Ogidan and fellow prostitutes
81 to 11 vote
73%: two-thirds of 109
Nobody says:
The lynchers are stainless
Like the calico or linen

Florie's florid of tears
The last to walk the Emperor
Out of office and grace
Oh! The heaviness of poli-machinations,
The Macbeths and Brutus of Africa.

When you were sober with brilliance
If all the hairs on our heads
Were tongues,
They would not have sung enough
Of your praise in honey flavored tunes.

Ikoyi, Lagos

The disobedient fowl

Only God says, "I am"
And He is
Only God boasts, "It is me"
And it is
Not Chube Ogidan.
The Ogbuefi* of his State
Boasts to defend him
A ₦200 million kitty.
The bravado
The bravura
The bold face
The chest beating
All a package of fallacy named corruption
A game face in spite of the obvious
The micro-dot place, the failure chain
Of Ogidan in history
Now that he is impeached–
However mischievously.
A mess in the Savannah
But an intransigent fowl
Obeys willy-nilly in the pot of soup.

Ilorin, Kwara State

---

* Ogbuefi — state executive

Gbajumo

One, decked and honored.
Does not tangle own community
A person of exposure
Does not provoke that which
Impugns integrity
That's the parable of Gbajumo—
One who 200 eyes recognize.
Rides phantom jets of flair
Basks the harmattan blaze
Brims the equatorial squall
Sits on the summit
Close to the cliff.
The ethical trough—
Kilometers deep under his feet
His siblings dined aristocracies
Wore caps of distinction and wizardry

Of course seasons and weathers change
Human praise changes too
Should never depend on it
It may not last.
Multitude feet of free-loaders
At the gate of the free giver
For the world knows fondly
Only the famed and endowed
But contempts for the have-nots—
Nobody licks from their plates.
People in times of ill wind
Bend southwards from the stem
Instead of the coconut leaf to be supple
It chooses to remain stiff
One does not have a tree on one's own farm
Without knowing what fruits it can grow.
Twinship of fame and infamy,
Is the apportionment of fate.

Ibadan, Oyo State

Birthday card for my country

Nothing works;
In the burning house of insufficiency
Headquarters of ding dong affairs
The moral ozone, the canopy of fair rectitude
Blazes to ashes and thin layers
A rainbow without its colours
Snails lost in its toxic deserts
Eagles without feathered propulsion
Lost height in the toxic wind
Instead, we sight trails of glow
Behind the comet of stench
Under it, we stand silhouetted
In the colour of pink.
We cannot hear the clamors of our grief
As we search blind folded, for
Pathways out of our grove.

Ibadan, Oyo State

The Songhai nation

Where eclipse of the mind
Hangs in the air of incorrigibility
Where the cattle-egret
Turns a messianic vulture
Where the skunk
Wears the deodorant of disguise
Where the sloth
Manages lions in distress
Where blood against blood
Course the same vein
Where each citizen, a parrot
Speaks the truth
The other knows as untrue
A cacophony of inimical national compositions,
When we shed tears only in one eye.

Agege, Lagos State

Mantras of the mafiosi

The nine orders of angels may not delay
Our windfalls
Or those that belong to others
The free booty of hope
From the otherness of situations—
A cultural polemic.
God died on the day
He birthed the Songhai Sinate
He forgot to give it a conscience
The magic of Mephistopheles
Secured their bank deposits without tellers
Strange activities went on there
We knew the villages of the wretches
Who just arrived in town yesterday.

Ibadan, Oyo State

Credentials

Some of those
Certified to legislate our lives
Have none of their own
The ethical swamp at the equator
How do you get diamond or gold
In the midst of rot?
The whole foundation a festering sore
A nation where magpies
Are kings.
Please remove them.
They overreach
Their inadequacy.

Agege, Lagos State

Debt relief mystique

Why should they care–
Mr. and Mrs. Third World?
What a beggarly mentality!
Yet,
Every rabbit boroughs sometimes
To roll backwards the stigma of history
But when the owl calls,
The day takes on the color of night.
Nothing western is free
The usual ethos of the First.
Never in business to lather
We borrow only to feed their crypts
And oil the crows amidst us
Billion oil monies swell their ranks
While the calibans eat penury for supper.
And hold destabilization for support
With daily nurture from our own devils
They both know how to tie the noose too tight.
Our wait for a debt relief
Is the very dance with death.

Lagos-Ibadan-Oyo Road

News — channel 10

Let us revise the past
To learn from it–
We hope.
Abacha regime and the like
Their national voice — NTA* lies
The unabashed authority of manipulation
Who trumpet the dictionary of distorts
Their index of fictions:
The government was immaculate
Its veins, quite transparent
The economy, very buoyant
The Head of State, simply strident
Until the coup of God struck
When he least expected.
That medium with a leprous tongue
A jaundiced crocodilian Cyclops
Does not know
Where it left its memory
For truth and decency.
Sanni was:
The solitary Commander of Dynamism
The very soul of Eternity
Cardiac arrest however nipped him
On the theater of libidinous activity
In a hotel at night
Now that he was forced to hell
The nation was reborn
NTA shines a renaissance
And many other siblings breathe on their own
To aid the farm of progress
The God of Justice never slept.

---

* NTA — Nigerian Television Authority, Ikoyi–Lagos

A tryst of the *Sinators*

A lampoon
A satire
A burlesque
A malaprop
A charade
The gold that rusts
Winks at its own demise
And brims at the steely iron.

There is no dawn yet
For our city of nights,
There is no sun yet
For our harmattan skies
There is no hope yet
For our wounded hearts
There is no zest yet
For our weary bones

If you have no new cloth
For the dead
Please do not remove
The one it wears now
The one that falls ill
May not suffer
The bludgeon of death.
Two hundred heads
May yet push away
The flood of poverty.
All we barter and banter
At the market devolve on money
A fire disaster acquaints one with fresh trees.
If you want to know a spoilt fish
Go ahead, smell the head.

Los Angeles, California

II

The Soul is Forever Longing

Three architects of the mind

One Norwegian
The other Danish
Me, the African
To board a plane
LA International
KLM, the bird
Destination: Amsterdam.
Only minutes as if ever
Before well acquainted
Hilarity infected and conjoined all
The beauty of a woman
Sometimes lies in the elegance of her tongue
Lines of vocation:
A maker of recycled materials
The other: A user of it,
To build structures, the nester
Me: The writer, selling words
To nest the mind,
Their nexus:
Builders of eco-reclaims
And architects of the soul,
Who make the earth worthy
For the living.

LA International, KLM 602, Los Angeles, California

Homecoming

In this pilgrimage
My eyes have seen
My emotions embraced
Pulses from high to low
Visceral reunions, a volcanic eruption
I have been a mental traveler, now home
Oh, I miss this land
The familiar haunts
The pastural rurality
The eternal silence of night
The chaos of the market place
The beauty of ugliness
The smiling poverty
The fresh beginnings
All say:
Welcome home
Of course, the oasis of executive ghettos too.

Much has changed
As much has not
My eyes of the world
These eleven years.
Sometimes, I am tired of civilization
So many cosmetized inanities
But here, physical penury inscrutable and unsmiling
The urban sprawls of blight
Some states the enclaves of peace
If only they are rich
Basic amenities will make a paradise
For the groundlings or hapless ninnies.
Their frowning faces
Speak poverty and frustration
Their feet pound the hardship trail daily

Welcome home to the mix
We have some ways to go.
My absence has been
The only connection between us to date.
Now, one appreciates:
The agonies of slow development
Or none at all.

Lagos

Okada motorscooters

Alternate rides in hell
Emergent solution to:
Prohibitive fares, overcrowding and leaky taxis
Delays without end—
Hence the convulsive agitations
To hop motorbike taxis called Okada.
Actually:
Accelerated journeys to hell
Rickety machines
Gulleys erosions engineered
Potholes where danger sneezes
The wear and tear—
Body and machine,
Clever twists and turns
Pedestrians incorrigible
What choice have they
On the pavements of inconvenience?
Very many scars on the mind
The hardships of poverty.

Mile 2, Lagos

An invincible melancholy

A look of artificial irritation
No matter the circumstance
Faces speak a nameless complaint
Even when the lip does not
No discernible logic at the instance.
With any utterance however,
The contours awake spasmodically
To complement the spoken thought
A look of artificial irritation—
It's many things:
In the crevice of time
All darkness and no sun:
Poverty without hope
Hardship with no relief
An inner landscape
With no oasis
Endemic auras of sadness
Wicked thoughts unspeakable.
The Euros or Westerners
Flash you a frosted smile,
As they pass you by.
Equally meaningless or vacant
But when Africans feel the tug of familiarity,
A sight of you—
All the continent aglow
Brimful and comradely
A little dose of happiness
Can change human temperament.

Vienna, Austria

Feel me with your eyes

Everyone hails you
When you are hale and hearty
But when you are ill
You are left alone on you own
That's the portrait of Lagos
Parts of it any way.

Chicago, its own blights
Los Angeles, her skid-rows
The roaches a New York invasion
The rats of St. Louis a jamboree
Lagos, her own wetlands
The last chapter of dreariness
The slush, the run-off, the shacks
Gutter defecations in plain view
Even in the roughages
A style of their own
Caked mattresses of dirt
Dried in the sun
Bugs swarming the surface
To escape heat and suffocation
Of the wetty foams
I felt like an alien
Waiting the corner
For a colleague visiting a family.

The youths live their pride in
Tattered, stylish clothings
Famous sport jerseys spring to view
—Michael Jordan—
Scotty Pipen, Orlando or Laker's Shaquill O'Neal
Life breathes even on the dung heaps.

Time recalls Manila.
The matted streets of Tijuana, Mexico,

Bogota and the Batustans of apartheid
The rich in their own ghettos.
When they need these pockets however,
Governments pass decrees
So skyscrapers can sprout out of the dirts.
Who says life is fair?
It favors only the rich and connected
Whoever listens to the moanings of the Talakawas*?

Lagos

---

* Talakawas — the poor

Book launching

The spate is alarming
Merit or no merit, the tubes deluged
The bees and the hornet
Every novice an author
Every dodo a writer
Every bat a diarist
Ever General a historian
Every financier a tycoon
Every politician an expert
Every riff-raff a bard
Every futurist a prophet
Every journalist an assessor
Every socialite a romantic
Every effete nob a swot
No difference between the chaff and the kernel
There is a catch though
A sanity to the insanities:
Business acumen
And
Social populism.
Most launchers in attendance
Are contract poachers
Their pay back checks sought
Three hundred million
Within an easy reach
A publisher's manna from the sky.
Never mind no one flips a page
Too busy licking their loots
Of course, their mistresses too.
When last did they read a page?
Money talks, influence obeys
Some of the press of course,
Their masters' tutelage.

Lagos

The facetious appeal

Whoever sows deceit
Will find sprouting in his own garden
Everybody knows that
A sieve lets water through
So, this desert mouse
Satellized his penury
At a book launching concourse
Each of 5 for one thousand dollars
He affected glancingly
He had not a cent in his pocket,
At such an august gallery
Of the world via the Internet too.
He meant well, though misguided
His appearance at the podium
Invited scoffs of derision
In the bid to impress.
Even the blind saw
Through his outfit
His account balance: was zero.
A man does not advertise
Himself as poor
The dehydrated cannot long hide
His emaciation.

Shylocks of the print
Will soon hound his trial to death
To put his pocket
Where his mouth had danced
With pomposity
Whoever trades in lies
Will pay in truth.
Many compatriots often pledge
As such, at public gatherings

To impress while their accounts
Starve with leakage
They never pay; fulfillment take to its heels
No honor without money.
Impatience with vanity brings out
What has been hidden.

NIIA, Victoria Island

Don't call me daddy

Reserved for my offsprings only
Here at home in Africa
To be so baptized,
Not only the ultimate regard
But also the ultimate jinx for capitulation
Sometimes forced willy-nilly,
Hastening it psychologically,
That's my point–
Intended
To place a gulf, between there and here

That's why I snapped.
Getting old or young: A state of mind–
Though I must admit
I was so ghoulish an apparition
The ravages of recent condition

Gaunt, scowly, and scrawny
Resisting the inevitable: A self deceit?
Please give me other labels–
That befit my waning ember.

Sounds vain but good
Not yet a cultural antiquity
But a psychedelic if you know what I mean
To give me the spunk
A dynamic that telegraphs knowingness
A usefulness, awareness, et al.,
Daddiness blurs everything
Places on you a mold
Not the sinew of time
I am not yet ready
To pack it up, don't rush me.

Lagos

Tijuana hearts of mercy

Dames:
Of Mexican descent
Eagle eyes of sweetness
Aztec gifts to the universe–
Val Trejo, Haidee Perez, and Yuri Palacio.
Three years of fellowship
A devotion beyond measure
A constancy for the centuries
Humanity: The Golden Rock
On which you anchor.
You share a puree compassion
Beyond the tongues of imagination
Heritage gave you the gift of beauty
Heaven, the vehicles of kindness
Aztec, the legacy of talent
The spirits, the diamonds of success.

You sport the gleeful inheritance of honesty
You remain straight like a tree
Warm like the depth of an ocean
Every cloth, made for its time
Your bond, made for eternity

I release you to warm heart of fate
And the magic hands of chance.
Your paths be paved with glory
Your marriage be cushioned with comfort
Your homes be painted with happiness
Your lives be stretched to eternity
For caring about me, this undiluted African

If I do not see you again
Remember the times we had
Of all your loves and reunions
Remember our own.

I bless you with my ancestral spirit
Our humanity, never to wear any colors
But the garments of worth and oneness
Adieu dear ones, Tijuana Princesses
Of Charm.

Chula Vista, California

Veronica Howard

This girl is a gem
A tower of kindness
At eighteen
God bless her dreams

And plans for the future
So sweet is she
Very much like a candy
Her inside
Glistens like a diamond
She remains an outpost of family
For all weary hearts
An old chap like me.
I thank you

Temecula-Riverside Highway

Indira Mann

Welcome to this earth, Indira
Your name already a beacon
In the ocean of nobility
Not only that–
A comet of history in front
Already blazes you a super star
Your parentage, a planetic mix
Of pith and presence
Your childhood dome–
Be painted with happiness.
Your adult-sphere–
Be strewn with success.
In your watershed of history
A brother already
The name of a millionaire:
Adnan K Mann.
Ancestral universe of Africa–
Soothes you.
Your life be sunny
And full of honey.
The substance of the orient
Be your inspirer
The world awaits
Your majestic pilgrimage.

San Diego, California

Folake & Jummy Bamigboye

Jumoke the older and
The social kite: slithe,
Suave, debonair, and sophisticated.
Folake, the swot—
With an inner mettle and
A painful inheritance of delight
Ambitious with uncanny thrusts of awareness.
Caught in the wind of a mental drama
To fly to the moon.
Her silence bears a sound
And wears the frock of meanings
You have the make
Of the world stage—
Ebonic and Sepian
Slim like the Sorghum plant
Quite a fit to find the sun.

Success is to never give up
To rise from the depth
You hibernated
Ancestral spirits look after you
For being the middle men
For my enterprises
The mental traveler
The clerk of time and consciousness
Drink me only with your minds.

San Diego, California

Akinnurun: the man of thunder

Olurombi* of legendary appeal
Skin-deep and heartfelt
If you need to know,
Just tease the tail of the lion.

I find the key
To unlock your smile:
Honesty and hard work.
Kingly and royal all the way
If anyone knows any different
Please let me know
Nothing happens by itself
But the hard work
That spreads the largesse of kindness

—Kolanut —
Your language of tradition
Always giving back to Ikaleland
One crowned with diadem of dignity
Never antagonizes his community
See his kudos from the fatherland:
The *Asojuoba* of Ikale
The *Bobajiro* of Oshoro
The *Sobaloju* of Ode Aye
The *Lumogho* of Idepe,
The *Baba Ijo* of St. John's Anglican

If a great man's name is hallowed
We strike the ground with a sword
As a mark of respect
One's work

---

* Olurombi — a person of exquisite appeal in African folklore

Lives after one's name.
Prostrating is the language
Of dignity that nobility appreciates
The one fit to blow the tusk
The trumpet of fame and awareness.

San Diego, California

Dorcas Ogunro: the Lubokun matriarchy

Grand matron of the Omogbehins
Grand conscience of royalty
We hear the music of your steps in our dreams
You gave us the rain which like the soil
Nurtures our fruition
Without you, where shall we be?
Your love gave us a shocking delight
In the quiet sessions of our thoughts.
Many of us your great grandchildren
Know you by name and the faith of history
Your handiwcrk in us, permanent
Shining the glory of our beginnings
We are what you put into us
Our face: your antique mirror
No word to describe your innocence
Contentment dances across our face
Little did you know
From marital pilgrimage out of Ilesha
Your seeds would green the earth
Every where your mustard seed
Every sphere your magic steps
Your space, the language of peace
Our trees ever grow to the sky.
One with children never dies.

This song, our golden tongues
To your matriarchal service
Our daily prayers in your remembrance
If we were stars
We would have stayed the galaxy with you
To carry the flags of memories
To a world that ignites discords.
Our enemies are enveloped by grief
Despair freezes their imagination.

La Jolla, California

The alien plant

The maiden visit home
These eleven years
Generates a commotion–
Absence had been
The only connection:
Is a he?
Is a she?
They argue on the street
The special hair fix
With a coxcomb
As if a James Brown
Strange as a UFO
Blame it on the accident
That forced the style
Where not much changed from tradition
As if this ghost not one of their own
Friends pinched or hailed the other
To gawk a phantom
The faddish-fiend from a never-land.
I do not mean to be alien
You feel sorry their perplexity
And the culture of limitation.
Not common, if not a taboo
To be different in the land of restrictions.
The feats of technology
To make self perfect or better groomed
They will never know.
We are doomed,
The day we all think or look alike.

Badagry Expressway

Musa Na'Allah*: an alley cat with eight lives left

He has been hit by a stroke
Pummeled by cancer
Speared by glaucoma
Harpooned by pneumonia
Racked by diabetes
Smothered by hypertension
Daggered by incontinence
Harrowed once by vertigo
Pokered by a heart murmur.

Now, cleared by angioplasty stenting
Of the brain
Re-aligned by radical surgery
Of the prostate
Each visitation is like
Pouring gasoline on a fire
All the time he was sinewed
With affection and care.

Are you still breathing?
His doctors wondered.
What a Cat,
With eight lives left!
He whispered: Faith my man, Faith
And medi-ingenuities in alien hands
He admits willy-nilly.

He is so well repaired
And over tuned up
Like a car throttling anew.

---

* Na'Allah — an instrument of God

Should have kicked the bucket
A long moon ago.
The bull* remains a lion
All over
Do not expect his obsequies soon
The gods are not asleep.

Los Angeles, California

---

* Bull — Na'Allah is a Taurus in zodiac designation

III

Whoever Despies Small Things Has Never Before Stepped on a Scorpion

Wanted

Wanted: I am lost
Anyone who finds me
Should please let me know.

La Jolla, California

College without convenience

This last chapter of the Third Worldness
A college, K-Poly that is
Five thousand strong and vast, the campus
Has no convenience anywhere
Since its genesis 25 years before,
On a visit, I had need.
You can imagine!
My students there
Now Chief Developers of the Mind
Fell on their faces:
Confession now compulsory
Not only necessary
"No such facility, Prof.,
Not a single one all, these years.
We live it in silent discomforts."
Students—men and women,
Future leaders so indecently deprived
Amazing Amazing!!
This is how the Proprietor, the government
That is, nurtures its seeds
A reflection of its own values.
These plants, flowers and fronds
Have to make do with the bush nearby
Imagine Imagine!!

Come on!
This, a crisis
Of environmental hygiene,
Not a privilege but a right
To live in human decency.
How will the State Assembly feel
Without restrooms in its premises
Or the Governor on his own?

If one were to fell a tree
In the bush,
One would gauge how it feels
If it were oneself being cut
Wake up, people!
This is the new millennium.

Kwara Poly, Ilorin

A marital college

My wife scores me a C
For my monthly tithe
That fetches the bacon
The starving writer's mite
An incomplete for my laziness
Very considerate she was
D for private moments
No longer an Olympian of 18
My daughter gives me a 7 for fatherhood
What does she care at 10?
I can be a complete Dad only
If I have more dough for fun.
The mother earns a ton
But her candy bag
Travels every month-end
Tradition then, my pony show.

My nature has the radiance of the sun
A certain breeze of peace
That calms the frayed nerves.
But they should wait
Till time ravages my breath.
They won't have me
To kick around any more
The household, their beautiful emptiness.

Amsterdam, Holland

The iron-hearted

Yoruba Version

Ki-ngbo-kingba
O loun o se mo
Akintola Taku
Olokan lile

Translation

Ms. Irrepressible
Who never agrees with anything,
Declares never again
Her signature of rebellion
Like Akintola, the iron-hearted
You know who,
My wife, Ms. Congeniality.

George's love

The Katwoman
Dreams of her George silly
Demobilized by his absence
Fills her lungs with his air
Lucky George
Where are you?
He too remains sleepless in his daze
In the US Navy craft.
They seem an item
The meeting point of two circles
When time reunites however,
Three days too long
Before a nuclear explosion
Only nature understands the logic of amorous feeling.

Vista, California

Ximena Munoz

Just met you, a morning flower in the sun
The horse does not graze
On the grass under it
An opportunity
Which is the beginning of a long tomorrow
Thanks for the warmth of your heart
Like the depth of an ocean on the equator
Let's anchor on motionless mutuality
Your smile infects my happiness.

Chula Vista, California

Philosophic inscriptions on Songhai buses

Sorry Lady, no time for love
No food for a lazy man
Remember your six feet
Behold I will do a new thing
Never begrudge others their destinies
Covered by the blood of Jesus
I stretch my palm in prayer
No one knows tomorrow
No money, no friend
Why worry when you can pray
Life goes on
A kiss does not show on the face
Life waits for nobody
No true friend
Monkey de work, baboon de chop
Life is full of determination
Water has no enemy
Be yourself, no compromise
No victory, no equality
A freeloader's job
Is never done on time.

Ebute Metta Bus Station, Lagos

The african time

My late Uncle for example,
Never was on time for any meeting
Or his international flights
Despite repeated alerts
The secretary's labor of reminders
As if time never ticked
His political reverie first
A jollity of sporty feelings
A hearty camaraderie of hopes.
Believes eternally,
The plane would never leave on time.
Many a time,
When he made it to the airport
The plane was climbing halfway to the sky.
Possibly, was late to Heaven too.

A gesture of bodily pang
The usual philosophy of regrets
Fate did not wish it to happen
Witches and wizards put to shame
His art of blame shifting
The fox blames the trap
Never himself
Others' faults, never his own

We play the catch up roulette
Mostly behind in everything
This has to change
Indiscipline is not our twin,
If not, we'll belong
In the Coward's Hall of Shame
Our incompetence or the irresponsible.

Nigerian Institute of Int'l Affairs, Victoria Island, Lagos

For Tayo Olafioye
(By Tunde Lee Asaju, Newswatch, Nigeria)

A thousand hoes,
A thousand matchets
Rebelled against the majestic mountains
Yet the mountain ate not
The mountain drank not
Neither did it wrap its body
In any form of clothing
But the mountain emerged victorious.
If it is a child that mentions your name in death
The food girds sand under its feet
Let them be grounded into a pulp
Be it male or female
That wishes you dead
Gradually, the food grinds the earth
May they be grounded into a pulp

The age brings strength to the antelope
The day the antelope becomes strong
The date of its death is changed
May you live, a thousand years
May the enemies converge
But may they be grounded in a pulp

A thousand years for you
Would amount to one day
The snail does not build its house
And fail to fill it up
The snail does not build a bigger shell
Until it is ready to fill its entirety
May you fill your position
Until you are ripe and ready.

Abuja

Beauty on water

(By Amos Ola Olafioye)

Pride of the North
Island of mermaids
Beauty on water.
The domicile of blonds
I doff my hat.
Your precious heart
Located on water
Vampires rove and prowl stealthily
The hungry cannibals
Lucifers on parade
Guillotine stares
Oh Lord!
Have mercy.
But the secret homes of infidelity
Convergence of iniquity
Congregation of mediocrities
A display of arrogance
Incipient irresponsibility.
Intellectuals and achievers
Geniuses and hybrids–
Flee from you.
Strangers "Mauvais sujet"
Remnants, a scapegrace
Prophets of doom
Antagonists of boom.
Revenge is a delight
Oppression of the meek
Only the strong survive.
You spit fires of words
"Godzilla" in ambush
Humming devil's own melody

An extreme venom
"Ecraser l'nfame"
Exhibition of discrimination.
A lonely night with you
Another pleasurable ride
To irreparable destruction.

Sweden

Prisoners of history

We are all prisoners of history
Only truth and reconciliation:
Our retrieval.
Difficult to be alone with time.

You won't know,
Where you are going
Until you know
Where you have been.

Exposing the truth
Goes to the heart of issues.

The truth of the past,
However ugly,
Heals the future.

What are we about?

Crimes against humanity:

Epical slavery in diaspora
Holocaust in Hitlerism, 6million roasted
Apartheid of South Africa, a people's denigration
Pol pot, the million skulls of Cambodia
The Philippines—never to forget Japan
Korea, the sex slatterns of the Emperor
Interments: the "Japs" in America
Yankee slaves in Asia
Polish Jews—the 16,000 massacres
To whom the Pope apologized not long ago
20 million Russians–
Stalin and Hitler sacrificed
The ethnic cleansings of Kosovo
Albanians, dispossessed and dislodged

Birmingham bombers of hate, 1963
4 black girls and the House of God pulverized

Jews and gentiles of Biblical
Proportions in Egypt
Just a tip of the iceberg
Vatican, the Janus
Always looking away

Even today
Some of the past still remains
Conscience always shattered
By events of the past.

Who will atone?

My son,
Confession and acknowledgement first
Then, forgiveness:
The only suitable exchange
For our lost humanity.
Without forgiveness
There is no future
Though nothing can ever
Compensate pain.
Admission is our feel-good tonic
Twin sister of therapy and apology.
We deceive ourselves
If we think we know who we are
Without it.
Someone must atone
And
Someone will accept and appreciate
Truth alone is no substitute for justice
But reconciliation is
Our self retrieval.
Events do not often die a permanent death
They relive across generations

Faulkner says:
History is not what was but is
And
Whoever accuses all humanity
Can only find one guilty.
Without forgiveness
There is no tomorrow
Though some long ago deeds,
Deserve punishment
That we may never forget
Moving on we must
As the earth around the sun,
Oh, Copernicus

Johannesburg, South Africa

Synopsis: The Year 2000 in Nigeria

The poets mind's presents a meteorological journal that measures the mood of his nation and, by a pathological inference, his own. The troubled life of his society writes a satiric, verbal music with a fado refrain inside his heart. He sees a cinematic motion of events as if a dream without time. Language, therefore, provides his last recourse or tool of consciousness when he wakes up from his mental torpor of disbelief. He must alert the future so that the past may not spawn again if only humans would learn from experience. God never gave them the gift of long memories, despite the sleep the sleeplessness of history. The poet therefore, stands forth as the watchdog to howl warning and the clerk to record time. The poet, consequently, follows the busy bee that forsakes no time for folly. His art forms the patrimony of humanity; his poetry — a labyrinth of hidden meanings.

After 40 years of independence, Nigeria remains a stillborn child. One who knows no saviors does not practice dying. I had thought that by now her midwives would have perfected their art of delivery. Rather, our land is still floundering in the dark, batty and ratty, as if born just yesterday.

Many great men and women, timbers of knowledge and moral rectitude like the mahogany, fostered folly, unbelievable in the annals of common sense, which we now know, follows not as commonly as the name suggests. They allowed the cyclone of moral pollution to bend their stems, sway their branches, twirl and rattle their treetops. Only Satan knew what came over them in the parliament of folly. High erudition made them more stupid, thereby betraying the ideals of scholarship. Perhaps the cruelty of power, the flippancy of its transitoriness and the illusion of its grandeur blinded them. In a gritty society, unbridled ambition rode them like a wild horse. The insane views of political conspirators, their private blizzards of greed and inordinate societal insensitivity blinded them. They appeared naturally black outside, but they became unnaturally dark inside; the pitchy night would become lost in the depth of their chambers. These degenerate sons and daughters corrupted their national siblings.

We saw a salacious synthesis of decadence in what they wreaked on the poor, the little people, who, possess only their needs. There was so much blame to share, not only among the accused but the ruling class as a group, the pretentiously innocent. Nearly all, suffered collective attacks of corruption, intrigue and betrayal of polity. As the scripture puts it, all have sinned and have fallen short of the grace of God — VOTERS. They all need redemption.

They awarded contracts to the dead and themselves the living dead, and for that, a bullet each to their heads. They made millionaires of their mistresses, concubines and sycophants, and for that, a bullet each to their hearts. They gave "Christmas bonuses" in the millions to themselves, for no justifiable rationale, in the oven of penury and intractable poverties and for that, a bullet each to their throats. The poet wonders how much Jesus Christ will collect from the Nigerian Tax Payers for his birthday. It is better not to be born than to be born and not receive a chance to enjoy a decent existence or the fulfillment of life. No one can deodorize wickedness or selfishness. Let God forgive them after they suffer punishment, for they have created an epicenter of stress in an already decimated society, through the tremors of the military's maniacal visitations and ruinations, in the dungeon airs of the equatorial heat.

For this is what China kills and never forgives the betrayal of proletarian innocence and trust. Our leaders often forgot that the summit of power lies close to the abyss of failure and disgrace. They allowed greed, narrow-mindedness and myopia to suffocate the elasticity of their minds. They deserve death, for they have given the poppies of hell to our people who conversed with poverty when they browsed the ceilings before they fell asleep at night. These penultimate leaders raked, raped, killed slowly by attrition, suffocated or asphyxiated the people out of sufficiency and the fulfillments of life. Their crimes may not be apparent or obvious, but, certainly, they practised the culture of death, the culture of financial assassination, the assassination of their people's comfort and decency which every human deserves. Why should one family or an individual, a group, by virtue of malfeasance in office, rob others for themselves and their children? The meaning and duty of governance constitute organizing society and, in part, facilitating responsibilities for all. Those who deny this right to life apportion the fate of early hopelessness and death. These thieves contributed to the stunting of needy citizens and society alike because the heartless few misdirected needed resources to their own vaults. Ordinary staples for survival are so expensive these days in the country. Added to this monumental inconvenience, is the lack of water, light and petrol. The government fails all and itself. All we see is a myth of action, no matter who is at the helm. Incompetence reigns supreme, and endless state travels abroad, constitute an elixir with no tangible results or benefits, just the locusts and dinosaurs mowing the farmland. In this age of the Internet, technology and business, the youth of today without educational preparedness for life, must accept the script of existence from other hands. Education provides society's passport to growth. Society builds one's foundation for initiatives.

We have no Marshall Plan such as that which rebuilt Europe after the Second World War. We have nothing that is rebuilding Africa after the exploitation and ruination that Colonialism — Third World War — brought. Every modern technocrat, elite or politician who defrauds or takes advantage of his or her people brands himself a certified General in this colonial army of dispossession and ruin. We apply nothing but a cosmetic solution to the problems besetting our society. The world has eyes and the airwaves extend its ears. The World remembers the economic sinkholes and earthquakes inflicted on Africa by Mobutu, Bokassa, Idi Amin and Abacha. Their likes still curry power today. Shall we stop this role of victimhood and roll up our sleeves! Great people rise from the ashes of their fall if they learn to manage well. Nothing in life is free. Therefore, we need statesmen and stateswomen who think and act beyond their time, beyond their comfort, beyond their village, beyond their state, and beyond their constituency.

Each generation writes a line or a paragraph in a world book of words. Do not, my brothers and sisters, let us write our own bloody epitaph or put a wreath of black roses on our existence. Let us build on the significant achievements of those of conscience who went before. Great people learn from the past and build for the future. Let's be patient with democracy. Do not let us immodestly pretend to be lions when we behave like rats and bats. We must eschew egregious legacies. The flea begins to believe in immortality when it sticks to the neck of the giraffe. Do not let us be such appendages or dependants forever. As our first step we must clean house; we must render our habitat livable. We must accept no appeasements nor tolerate mediocrities. We must allow no more smut from above or below. Seaminess, seediness, steaminess do not count in our national character. Prove this wrong my compatriots.

www.ingramcontent.com/pod-product-compliance
Lightning Source LLC
Chambersburg PA
CBHW011944150426
43192CB00016B/2775